Alexandra Kollantai

Women's Liberation and Revolutionary Love

Sheila Rowbotham

Spokesman Books

First published in *The Spokesman* 4 & 5 (1970) and re-issued as
Spokesman Offprint No. 1 (1973).
This edition published in 2022 by
Spokesman Books
5 Churchill Park, Nottingham, England NG4 2HF

www.spokesmanbooks.org

ISBN: 978 0 85124 920 9

ALEXANDRA KOLLANTAI

WOMEN'S LIBERATION AND REVOLUTIONARY LOVE

Sheila Rowbotham

Many features of communism during the 1920's in the Soviet Union have since been buried so deeply in the dustbins of history that their rediscovery becomes a major resalvaging work. Not only have there been successive Soviet reinterpretations but the distortions which appeared in the West both before and during the Cold War make the whole process even more difficult.

Most confused are the questions of sexuality, the family and the emancipation of women. There is on one side the dark mutterings in *Pravda* in the 30's about petty bourgeois hooliganism and the depravity of the younger comrades, on the other innumerable horror stories about baby farms and the nationalisation of women. However, undoubtedly, in the years immediately following the revolution an extraordinary process of transformation of the inner relationships between people took place, which inevitably affected the position of women most radically.[1] The writings of Alexandra Kollontai are essential to any attempt to trace the course and clear away some of the ambiguities in this process. Unfortunately little of her work is translated into English and none which deals with the position of women is now easily obtainable.

However, despite this, a preliminary partial study is justifiable not only because she commented with exceptional perception on important aspects of the Russian revolution which have been ignored, but because so much of what she said is extremely relevant to the liberation of women now.

Communist Feminism

Her feminism was completely inseparable from her communism. The impetus towards both came closely together. She describes when she was young a vague feeling of "mission". She was uncertain exactly what she should do ... "but I wanted to fight against injustice, especially social injustice, and against brutality from those who had the power in their hands. Later I thought my mission was to struggle against unfairness in the sexual question."[2]

To understand the way in which these combined it is necessary to consider the movement before 1917 as well as the nature of the debate amongst the Bolsheviks after the Revolution.

The revolutionary political tradition into which she came as a young girl brought a natural theoretical unity to her emotional sense of the two missions. The emancipation of women was one of the aims of the radical intelligentsia, feminism appeared naturally within the body of theory which developed in the successive phases of the Russian political opposition movement in the late 19th and early 20th centuries. Organisationally women achieved, too, a degree of respect and independence, playing a heroic and exceptionally prominent part in the struggle against the Tsar. No separate liberal feminist movement in the sense of the suffragettes developed until long after feminist influences had had considerable effect within the general movement for social revolution. Kollontai describes this in the 1880's.

> "England had such strong and independent women as Mary Wollstonecraft and Florence Nightingale. We looked up to them in admiration hoping that there would come a day when even we would be able to open a door to new activities for women and our names become known for great social deeds. We admired John Stuart Mill for defending women's rights and popular books on Darwin's theory."[3]

In the years before the revolution, as she moved gradually towards the Bolsheviks her political understanding broadened and deepened in many directions. The 1896 textile strikes in St. Petersburg had an important effect. Her membership of a group of young writers studying marxism to which Lenin belonged, her study of educational ideas, of political economy and the influence of Kautsky and Luxemburg helped too. On the Bloody Sunday of 1905 she was out in the street. But her interest in the position of women continued. In 1905 the attempt of an emerging group of bourgeois feminists to involve working women in a non-revolutionary feminist movement which was intended to bring together on a common platform all the liberal political organisations, made it necessary for her to clarify the differences between their concept of emancipation and her own. She saw that unless this was done it would confuse and weaken the revolutionary case. "The women comrades of the Menshevik faction adhered, but I denounced such manoeuvres". During 1906 she managed to create a base by setting up a women's club with the help of a small group of comrades. These clubs were to appear frequently after the revolution. In the autumn of 1906 at the first Women's Congress in St. Petersburg both Mensheviks and Bolsheviks argued that a genuine social emancipation was impossible without revolution. By this time living underground she wrote *The Basis of the Woman Question,* a summary of her position on feminism in relation to marxism, before she had to flee. In exile her friendship and political association with Clara Zetkin and Rosa Luxemburg strengthened both her involvement in the women's movement and her inclination to emphasise theoretically the importance of mass participation, the significance of consciousness and human activity on political events. She also gained important practical experience through political work in several strikes in France. The most unusual of these was a strike in 1911 by housewives against the high cost of living.

She had approached the woman questions before, philosophically and historically, questioning the binding force of morality and examining the changes in sexual mores. Whilst she was still in exile she increased her empirical knowledge of the existing situation of women immeasurably. The Moscow group of the Social Democratic minority asked her to prepare a draft resolution for a protective maternity law to be presented to the Duma. Characteristically she began an exhaustive study of various systems of maternity legislation and the physical and psychological implications of motherhood. She finally published the results as a book *Society and Motherhood* in 1915. At the same time with Clara Zetkin, Kollontai was continually insisting that the fight for women's emancipation must be part of the party's programme.

All three of these emphases had an important effect after 1917. Although the club was closed Kollontai says in her *History of the Women Workers' Movement in Russia* that it "left indelible traces" in St. Petersburg. The women textile workers took militant industrial action before the revolution, and in February, 1917, women workers played a crucial political role. "They go up to the cordons more boldly than men, take hold of the rifles, beseech, almost command: 'Put down your bayonets – join us'." In October women were on the barricades.

The first All Russian Conference of Proletarian and Peasant Women in November, 1918, was a confirmation of the significance of the women's movement. It was agreed there should be no separate organisation of Bolshevik women but that there should be separate sections of the party, working groups, commissions and committees to struggle for women's emancipation.[4] The legislation which shattered the old patriarchal family provided further evidence of the Bolsheviks' seriousness on the question. Women were no longer subject to men before the law, divorce was made easy and the registration of a relationship was not obligatory. As Commissar of Social Welfare Kollontai organised the Institute for the Protection of Mothers and Children, which exerted an important influence on general maternity provisions as well as on the situation of women at work. Sixteen weeks' free care for women before, during and after pregnancy was introduced, expectant mothers did lighter work, could not be transferred or dismissed without the consent of a factory inspector, night work was prohibited for both pregnant and nursing women. Maternity homes, clinics and advisory centres were set up.[5]

These were dramatic and drastic changes in a country in which Tsarist family law had kept women in complete subjection. What is more they were changes which penetrated into the innermost forms of social living. For millions of women who had been subdued literally by the whip it was like a great awakening. The new consciousness penetrated far beyond the small groups of intellectual communist women and even beyond the working women in large towns. In 1925 Kayer Nissa, a girl of twelve from the Muslim East who had attended one of the women's clubs, being cast out of home, and supported in her studies by the women's section, spoke as delegate at a conference.

> "We have had enough of having our faces covered ... of being imprisoned, in stuffy ichkaris, sold at the tenderest age to old men, maimed in body and soul, and degraded to slaves."

Sometimes this new confidence made women criticise the Bolshevik men. In a discussion on divorce in the same year Comrade Shyropuva, a peasant woman, reminded the men comrades:

> "We are still in the dark, we were enslaved for centuries. All we know is priests' gossip - which we are only now beginning to forget about; 'The wife must fear her husband' ... Our men comrades they know a bit more than we do. You must teach us, you must not just laugh and giggle;

that is no use, particularly on the part of the enlightened comrades, the Party men. I do not consider this the way of comradeship ... To us that is very insulting."

More than this, people consciously created new forms of human relationships which enabled the revolution to take root in most practical places. The youth communes which grew up in the twenties and early thirties were amongst the most important of these communal-cultural associations. Not only were women freed from the traditional domestic work within the commune, but completely new ways of connecting to property and to people began to be defined. Some had a communal wages fund. They shared belongings. In the day books, communards expressed what was happening. Sometimes they complained. The old ways continued. " I have brought my electric kettle with me to the commune, but they use it carelessly. Why did I bring it? "But they looked after each other, the commune took on social responsibility for its members. Marya is depressed, Tanya not admitted to the university. They lived as a new family. Naystat in *Youth Communes* wrote:

"The new byt like the new family, will be able to grow up only when all the necessary economic conditions are fulfilled. For that reason it is not yet time to consider a complete reconstruction of life on a socialist basis ... We begin by building up the fundamental conditions of a socialised life, the commune is the model of the future socialist byt. But even now, marriage in a commune is different from marriage elsewhere. For it anticipates the marriage of a socialist society in that the economic tie has ceased to play a part in the mutual relations of husband and wife. The same applies to the question of the children, although the communes have little experience in this matter at present. During their early years the communes did not desire children for material reasons. But now there are a considerable number of commune children."

These experiments in co-operative living not only transformed the practical situation of women, they enabled them to conceive of themselves in a totally different way. In a women's commune in 1930 there was a saying: "The hen is a bird, a woman is a human being".

In 1928 in a youth commune in Moscow the group decided finally that marriage would not break up *the* co-operative but that the girl communard must enter in her own right, as Katja not as Vladimir's wife. When Katja applied she said, "I wish you to consider my case without any 'alleviating circumstances', I wish to become a regular member of the commune and not just the wife of a commundard". It was an important distinction. Wilhelm Reich in *The Sexual Revolution* describes how they reached different positions on the sexual question in the communes. Not surprisingly there was great confusion. Some attempted complete suppression. Others tried to create a new sex morality. But it was very difficult. One day Vladimir no longer loved Katja. He could not explain it to himself. The girls were angry. They said Vladimir is a pig. These questions did not seem to be covered in the marxist theory books.[6]

What was to be done?

Bolsheviks under the bedsheets

All Bolsheviks were not equally happy about the developments. While the emancipation of the woman in the work situation, educational opportunities and birth control were generally acceptable to many of them, there was more uneasiness about the abolition of the family and sexual liberation. This combined with a less explicit suspicion of the new political confidence of women.

Moreover there were great practical difficulties. In a debate of the Moscow propagandists in the early 1920's, complaints were made about the way old family ties were broken for new ones, and the new ones were "as fleeting as the old".[7] There was real concern. Peasant women, too, spoke of the lack of security which had resulted from the new laws in debates before the changes in the new family laws 1925-26.[8] There were definite contradictions in the new freedom which had been conceived in a completely different cultural situation when it was imposed on women in extremely traditional positions. Great hostility was aroused, especially in Muslim areas. In Uzbekistan, for instance, in 1928 there were 203 cases of anti-feminist murder.[9] Girls who went to the meetings of the women's clubs, wore bathing costumes and unveiled, were persecuted, too, in Baku.[10]

The conditions of scarcity and upheaval which resulted from the war made these problems greater. The housing shortage, for example, made privacy almost impossible. The effects of this were not just to produce physical discomfort but also psychological distress. Nor is the experience of revolution conducive to settled domestic unions. The great external transformations inevitably penetrated personal life. Experience kaleidoscoped, people moved away from each other.

It was extremely difficult to distinguish always the sources of the problems which arose, to understand what were long-term and what were short-term phenomena. In some cases, too, understanding was blocked by outright hostility. There were men no matter how revolutionary who wanted their wives to cook the dinner and not to go to meetings. It was most uncomfortable to find revolution in your own kitchen or in your own bed. People were rather afraid of the idea of revolution affecting them so intimately. It was felt there was something explosive and dangerous about such changes. There was direct sexual clash. Sometimes the women said to the men, "You only think about yourselves". Trotsky commented, "It is quite true there are no limits to masculine egotism in ordinary life".[11] Sometimes the women were afraid of the new developments. One reaction was to simply try and ignore what was happening or call it by other names. The functionary Koltsov complained:

"These questions are never discussed. It was as if for some reason they were being avoided. I myself have never given them serious thought, they are new to me. They are extremely important and should be discussed."

Similarly a comrade called Tseitlin said:

"In the literature, the problems of marriage and family, of the relations between man and woman, are not discussed at all. Nevertheless, these are exactly the questions which interest the workers, male and female alike. When such questions are going to be the topic of our meetings, they know about it and flock to our meetings. The masses feel that we hush up these problems, and in fact we do hush them up."[12]

It was all very embarrassing. No simple clear line could be taken. The feeling grew that these matters had nothing to do with communism. The writer of a standard work on Party Ethics, Yaroslavsky expressed this. "We don't want to be for ever looking under the bedsheets."[13] Lenin was more positive. He condemned the hypocrisy of the old bourgeois morality with its double standards and he realised the profundity and significance of the changes in personal relations. " New boundaries are being drawn." He stressed, "Communism should not bring asceticism". The problem was, of course, in what way were the new boundaries to be drawn. Lenin could see the danger of the rejection of tenderness and feeling which was simply a reversal of the old attitudes. He attempted to distinguish between what he called the glass-of-water theory which conceived "free" love as being simply the satisfaction of desire and the "free" communist union which implied deep feeling and comradeship.[14] Unfortunately instead of his conversation with Clara Zetkin being regarded as a way of helping people to make up their own minds, it very quickly took on the force of a new authority. People were in fact being ordered to be free. Inevitably it was to swing the full circle.

Every attack on the original changes from the mid- 30's and 40's quoted Lenin happily in justification of measures which were very far from his views either on the emancipation of women or on the form of communist unions.

There was an awkwardness on the question of love. This related closely to the problem about how much to accept and how much to reject from the pre-revolutionary culture. Romantic love in the western sense was so closely bound up with individualism. Communism was at once about real liberation and the socialisation of individual freedom. *"Love"* tended to appear as a rather unsociable emotion. One reaction was an ascetic austerity which denied emotional sexual feeling. The other response was to divorce sexuality from emotion. Both were flaunted as the new communist morality, though it was obvious that the genuine conception of such a morality could come only from a long period of cultural practice.

The immediate situation of war communism and the N.E.P. period complicated matters further. In the 1920's, too, it is clear that there was considerable generational conflict. For the older Bolsheviks the new ideas had been the product of great intensity and earnestness, in desperate situations where the margins of choice were narrow and the penalties for negligence and superficiality severe. The younger Communists inherited a tradition and redefined themselves in relation to it. Quite a lot they took for granted. Their parents seemed very ponderous about their free unions. Everything now was more relaxed. The older Bolsheviks looked on in horror at what seemed to them a casualness and impersonality in personal relationships which shocked them. There was a tendency amongst the young to dismiss love contemptuously. Sex was as simple as going to the cinema.[15] The older generation reacted impatiently when they were accused of "survivals of a Social-Democratic attitude and old-fashioned philistinism" on the sex question. Lenin can't have been alone in his snorts of indignation against "yellow-beaked fledglings newly-hatched from their bourgeois tainted eggs".

The real failing of the Bolshevik orthodoxy was the inability to criticise particular manifestations of the sexual movement, while retaining a positive and affirmative approach towards the liberation of personal relationships. Though Lenin was well aware of the necessity for marxists of comprehending the sexual social process in its totality he was capable of an intellectual narrowness very foreign to the rigour he applied to other subjects. "I mistrust sex theories" ... opened the way for a fatal refusal to engage with bourgeois psychology in a creative rather than a dogmatic way.[16]

Consequently the tendency was to focus on particular areas in which women achieved a greater freedom and opportunity for development. Some partial manifestation of emancipation would be recognised, isolated and praised, but then the implications and interactions would not be followed through. The most simplistic was the quotation of endless statistics which showed women were participating in productive labour. Not only did these often tend to gloss over the fact that much of this was unskilled, but they frequently failed to answer the crucial questions about how this affected the consciousness of the women, or how this in turn influenced their domestic living. Trotsky's approach in *The Problems of Life* connecting the liberation of women from the household with the question of initiative and organisation from below and the creation of new forms of communal living, was much more considered. But he drew short at the psychological oppression in sexual and emotional life. When there was a revival of interest in the ideas about the withering away of the family in the early period of the first Five Year Plan, the emphasis was not so much on the position of women and the creation of personal communist consciousness as on potentiality which was released for mass participation *in* work. For example, A. M. Sabsovich who belonged to the "leftist" deviation was much more involved in the sheer efficiency of abolishing the family rather than in the redefinition of psychological boundaries in the relations between people.[17]

Communism and Love

Amidst all this the muffled voice of Alexandra Kollontai provides a crucial perspective. Much of what she said was neither unique nor new, but she maintained the tension between these various aspects of emancipation in a particularly balanced way. She refused to isolate any particular area of experience, and she refused to cordon off certain regions of consciousness as danger points it was forbidden to explore. To understand her significance it is necessary to see both how she continually connected her feminism to her communism, and how she followed ideas through to the furthermost consequences of things. It was this connecting and following through, rather than simply the content of what she said, which made her ideas at once heretical, embarrassing, and revolutionary.

The way in which her feminism merged with her communism has already been mentioned. She always related also the liberation of women to the freeing of men. In a critique of the bourgeois feminist movement, she pointed out how they failed to do both of these:

"From the start these advocates of feminine rights in the bourgeois camp never even thought of a new social order as offering women the widest and only firm basis of their emancipation. Socialism was alien to them ... imagining themselves to be the advocates and spokesmen of the demands and aspirations of all women, believing themselves to be above class differences ... while endeavouring to imitate the man in every possible way, they kept strictly apart and opposed the interests of women to those of men."[18]

Her opposition to their position is thus political in a double sense. She criticised at once their aims, and their belief that they were "above" class, and the way they restricted the possibilities of any genuine emancipation of women, by at once borrowing from the bourgeois man, and making "Man" in an abstract the enemy. This ignored the economic and social changes which were necessary for the freeing of all women rather than a privileged minority. They tried to by-pass social revolution.

The first conditions for such a revolutionary freedom were economic independence, improvements in education and training, social security and liberation from the drudgery of housework. "Separation of kitchen from marriage was as important a principle as the separation of Church from State".[19] She looked to the various schemes which were being tried or discussed to solve this – better work conditions and education, collective housekeeping, public restaurants, associated kitchens, laundries, clothes mending centres, nurseries, kindergartens, children's colonies. All these would mean, "The working woman will no longer be obliged to sink in an ocean of filth or to ruin her eyes in darning her stockings or mending her linen."

The new freedom was not some distant abstraction, it was something which affected particular people in a real way at home. She stressed always that the outward form of law should relate to the real situation. There was considerable controversy on the question of alimony.[20] At first both partners had to pay. But then many women complained. The law placed an unregistered relationship on the same terms as a registered one. But sometimes women became pregnant after casual intercourse. Then there was the problem of responsibility for the children. At a public debate in 1925 she said: "For that reason it is impossible under any circumstances to bring the matrimonial relations of the sexes within a legal formula - so long as there are workers' barracks, and a housing shortage and so many half-grown children running about without supervision." She suggested a general insurance fund or "common pot" to supplement individual contributions to alimony.

But she was criticised by factory women on the grounds that what one man did was no other man's business. They agreed there should be no distinction between registered and unregistered marriages. But the "common pot" would merely encourage seducers. "For if once a man has succeeded in fooling a woman with poetical spells and African passion and begetting a child with her, then he should pay his 'third'. He will take care to avoid a second 'third'. For even one third is bitter experience."[21]

It was clear this practical liberation could only take effect with the creation of a new consciousness amongst women.[22] Alexandra Kollontai understood only too well the women's conservatism. Many were afraid of their new freedom; they were accustomed to seeing the man as "provider". It seemed as if the revolution was taking away their security. They tried to cling on to their own "pots and pans". They thought the communists wanted to tear their babies from their arms. It was no good lecturing the women on revolutionary commitment, a tendency of some of the comrades. It was necessary to remove rather the objective factors which gave rise to the fear, insecurity and dependence. She pointed out for example, "If under the bourgeois system a women was anxious to please her bread-winner huband with her cooking, it was precisely because he was in fact the breadwinner. In a Workers' State, however, where woman is recognized as an independent unit and citizen, it is doubtful whether you would find many volunteers for stooping over a stove to win a husband's approval." The consciousness of independence came with the experience of it.[23]

But this was only half the problem. The other half was sitting down and demanding its dinner. Not only did husbands want the old pre-revolutionary housekeeping, but they had been known to throw papers of the Women's Department on to the fire because they resented the time their women spent in political activity. It was necessary for the men to discover a new consciousness as well as the women.

Kollontai realised this implied in fact a domestic revolution. The personal structures within which people related to each other had to be transformed along with the revolution in the political and economic structures. Here the legislation which affected the family was all-important. She was aware of the immensity of these changes. In *Communism and the Family* she wrote, "The entire organisation of the proletarian family is being organised in a manner which is so new, so unaccustomed, so 'bizarre' as to have been impossible to foresee."[24]

Nor did she underestimate the new problems which arose. But she saw clearly the connections between the bourgeois family and the old values of subordination and domination, and property feelings between people.

"The capitalists themselves are not unaware of the fact that the family of old, with the wife a slave and the man responsible for the support and well-being of the family … is the best weapon to stifle the proletarian effort towards liberty."[25]

New kinds of collective domesticity were not seen simply as a means of relieving women, or of changing their position within the family, they were essential for the growth of new relations between men and women. But Kollontai went further in emphasising the interpenetration of the inner and outer worlds, and the need to create new forms of living for the personal as well as the political and economic life. She saw new cultural forms as a means of communist education, as a way of creating through personal practice new values, not as ideas in a book but from the experience of living them. Such an emphasis was extremely significant politically. The heroine of her novel *Free Love,* discussing the house communes with a rather bureaucratic party member, says they must be transformed from short-term solutions to the housing shortage into "schools and foster the Communist spirit". He was completely bewildered, regarding education as something that belonged to school and university, and nothing to do with housing methods.[26]

At this point the link between her early interest in educational theories and her feminism emerges. She was in harmony with an important tendency in educational thought in the Soviet Union in the '20s which saw education in the future communist society as completely integrated in social life and prophesied the withering away of the school. This approach, which fell into disrepute from the mid-'30s, was part of a general libertarian educational trend which criticised knowledge as a rarefied commodity and the teacher as authority.[27]

There is also an obvious connection between her thought in relation to the emancipation of women and her analysis of the growth of bureaucracy which appeared in the pamphlet *The Workers' Opposition.* The new forms of living only had an educative role when they came from the initiative and participation of the people concerned. The abolition of the bourgeois family and the destruction of the old values could no more be effected by order from above than communism could be introduced by decree. While this was understood in theory, so often it was passed over in practice. She describes the process by which this growth of self-activity was hindered. Workers tried to organise new schemes of communal living, dining-rooms, day nurseries and other schemes. They found these were blocked with red tape and officialdom. They became bitter, shrugged their shoulders and said, "If that is the case ... let officials themselves take care of us". This was happening on a much larger scale in the administration of the party. People were not able to feel responsible anymore. "Some third person decides your fate. That is the whole essence of bureaucracy."[28]

The problem was of course the less accustomed people were to running their own lives the quicker they gave up and the sooner decision-making passed to "some third person". In *Free Love* she describes how this happened with working women. Often they didn't know how to speak up for themselves and consequently found they were ignored or ridiculed. But the heroine Vasilissa, a knitter, always managed to stand up for herself.

"Other female workers used to find themselves embarrassed, but Vasilissa could always, when necessary, and without first having to think about it, assume the talking. And always she spoke practically. The other comrades tended to think the women's problems were not worth bothering about. Women's affairs appeared always more trivial to them than general matters. People were accustomed always to take that view, and thence there resulted the backsliding of the women."[29]

Thus just as the workers decided to leave communism to the officials, the women dropped back easily into the assumption that politics were the business of men.

It is clear then that not only was her feminism part of her communism but that the emphasis in both were the same. Obviously she did not conceive or express these ideas in isolation. There was a strong tendency in the party which emphasised the importance of self-activity, spontaneous initiative and participation as opposed to communism by decree. But Kollontai had a particular and awkward knack of crystallising these rather vague feelings and acting upon them. This literal characteristic, apparent in her role in *The Workers' Opposition,* infuriated many people before Lenin denounced her as a threat to the unity of the Party.[30] For instance, a very different critic, one of the supporters of the Kerensky government who had held the post Kollontai took in the Department of Social Welfare, commented in disgust: "This absurd Madame Kollontai invites the servants to come and sit in armchairs at her meetings. What can they know of social reforms or of technical training. It is putting the feet up and the head down quite mechanically."[31]

In fact the lower civil servants proved invaluable allies with their detailed experience, and their willingness to work long hours with her. Madame Kollontai continued her policy of upsidedownness not only in the way she regarded the women's movement but in the way she went about organising women. She told Louise Bryant the revolutionary government had a tendency to overlook women. It was therefore vitally necessary to develop in them a consciousness as a group to prevent this. Women's Congresses were extremely important not simply for the political work they did but for the way they increased women's confidence and feelings of importance. The peasant woman who had been to a Women's Congress returned to her village with pamphlets, posters and a new status.[32] The educational women's clubs developed along similar lines under her guidance.[33] Her insistence that the emancipation had to come from women was not without contradiction. Some Bolsheviks hoped to free the women in the· Muslim areas by persuading the men gradually to allow women more freedom – but not Kollontai. She told Louise Bryant:

"I have been laughed at ... because so far I have brought ... only a few women from the harems of Turkestan. These women have thrown aside their veils. Everyone stares at them, they are a curiosity which gives the congresses a theatrical atmosphere. Yet all pioneering work is theatrical. It was distinctly theatrical when the audiences used to throw eggs at your pioneer suffragettes ... How else would we get in touch with Mohammedan women except through women."

The problem was of course that Kollontai's women were immediately ostracised, losing their homes and their husbands because the contrast between the old domination and the new liberation was so extreme. But certainly they emerged understanding what the revolution was about.[34]

This upsidedownness gave her a reputation for heresy which has saved her from the ranks of our "noble Soviet women". Indeed according to Angelica Balabanoff who worked with Kollontai in the women's movement during the early years of the revolution, "she was a frequent source of both personal and political annoyance to the party leaders. On more than one occasion the Central Committee had wanted me to substitute for her in the leadership of the women's movement, thus facilitating the campaign against her and isolating her from the women of the masses". Angelica Balabanoff says she realised what was going on and refused.[35]

If the way Alexandra Kollontai combined her feminism and her communism embarrassed party leaders, much more disturbing was her tendency to explore the subjects which were "never discussed". In the preface to *Free Love* (sometimes better translated as "Red Love") she wrote:

"This novel is neither a study in morals nor a picture of the standard of life in Soviet Russia. It is a purely psychological study of sex relations in the post-war period. Many of the problems presented are not however exclusively Soviet Russian; they are world-wide facts which can be noted in all countries. These silent psychological dramas, born of the change in the sexual relations, this evolution, especially, in the feelings of women, are well known to the younger generation."[36]

It is this "purely psychological study of sex relations", this interest in "the silent psychological dramas", this connection to an international sexual revolution, and the examination of the "evolution, especially, in the feelings of women" – young women, too – which made Kollontai unusual and necessarily suspect. Left Communists who wrote about the withering away of the family in a far away distant society upset no one. Communist feminists who concerned themselves with what particular women were experiencing at that moment upset many.

The plot of *Free Love* is simple. Vasillissa, a knitter, forms a free union with Volodia, an ex-anarchist, who becomes a member of the party and takes on a job as director of a large industrial concern. He has an affair with Nina, a non-political ex-bourgeois woman who is very beautiful. Eventually Vasillissa leaves him. However the real interest in the book is the four conflicting themes which run through it and the tensions behind them. At one level there is a political clash. The first signs of a break between the two appear in their very different ideas about politics, not in their original theoretical argument about centralism which was only superficial, but a much deeper difference about the extent to which commitment to the revolution penetrates the way you live. Vasillissa was distressed by her husband's liking for a grand style of living which involved dubious deals during the N.E.P. period with non-party bourgeois. This explodes with particular intensity when some of the workers under her husband complain about working conditions. They come to the great house of the Director and start talking to Vasillissa. She forgets her role as his "wife", becomes her old Bolshevik trade union bargaining self again, and begins excitedly to plan ways for them to fight back. He returns, sees this, and furiously drags her inside. At another level as they move away from one another the relationship becomes increasingly dishonest. When she finds he has secretly slept with Nina she feels he has done wrong not in going to another woman but in deceiving her about it. At the same time she is jealous of Nina, who possesses the traditional attributes of women, beauty and elegance. She begins to feel her union with Volodia is a charade.

> "There was no longer comradeship, no longer affection, between them ... She was wife in the house merely to serve as hostess, to act as a cover. I live, she said, in wedlock with a Communist. but another woman is the wife for delectation, for love in a secret little house."

At the same time Kollontai explores the way in which it is impossible for Vasillissa to retain her old independence. She has only a borrowed existence as his wife, she no longer has her work, especially her political work in the factory and the party. When she tries to leave him she says, "I have panted enough in this cage, I have played the Directress enough ... Take for a wife one of those who value such a life."[37] When she finally goes she throws off "a skin which did not fit me."[38]

But in fact the skin held her to him for a long time. Kollontai brings out the clash between the struggle for identity and the ties which had developed over the years when they were together, as well as the very real sexual passion. At first her sexuality was in harmony with the other ways she communicated with him. But ultimately there is opposition between the desire he can still arouse in her and their obvious incompatibility. It is as if her sexuality might swamp her separate identity. The political, emotional, intellectual and sexual factors combine. The only solution is to leave him. But Vasillissa's choice simply ignores the basic causes of tension. She goes away, and is able to rid herself of her jealousy of Nina the traditional feminine, in an understanding mixed with compassion. She has a child and plans to rear it "in the community way", co-operatively. She finds her identity thus only by denying the existence of the man and her own sexuality. The only solution possible is no real solution.

But this was precisely what Kollontai meant by *Free Love*. She wanted to "... teach women not to put all their hearts and souls into the love for a man, but into the essential thing, creative work. When I look through my works I can see that it was this aim that inspired most of my writing on the sexual question. Love must not crush the women's individuality, not bind her wings. If love begins to enslave her, she must make herself free, she must step over all love tragedies, and go her own way."[39]

It was a negative freedom. A freedom of nonattachment which tended to appear in feminist thought in the period. There was a sense in which very strong personal emotion almost inevitably appears in opposition to the liberation of the women because traditionally such emotion bound women. But this tended to force women to accept that emancipation meant denying part of themselves. When Kollontai was writing it seemed as if this was the only way out. Unfortunately the tendency could result in a dismissal of the personal and sexual dimensions in relationships. There is a trace of the stiff upper lip. Just as Kollontai could share the easy optimism characteristic of communists in the period – that "intelligent educators" would somehow escape the taint of the past and teach the values of solidarity and comradeship in their revolutionary purity- she shows a hint of that self-denying strain which simply cut itself off from awkward emotion very common in the revolutionary movement. The rejection of the cellular individualism and the passionate egotistic possessiveness of the bourgeois family came to imply the necessary superiority of external social activity to the inner personal life. Such a rejection which arose naturally from the need for intense political commitment in the revolutionary period, was elevated into an impossible and restricting moral principle.[40]

It was not that Vasillissa should have continued a relationship which became only formality, but that the points of tension, the struggle of the woman for independent identity in relation to the mad and the apparent contradictions between her intellectuality and her sexuality are too facilely resolved. Such questions were and still are crucial.

In *Love of Three Generations,* the young communist Zhenia tries to solve the problem by divorcing strong emotion from her sexuality. She slept with two men at the same time and was in love with neither. The situation was complicated by the fact that one of them was her stepfather. She told her mother, "But I liked them and I felt they liked me .... It's all so simple. And then it does not tie you down to anything."

She argued with her mother, who was shocked, that there could be nothing wrong in this as "I did it voluntarily and willingly. As long as we like each other we remain together; afterwards we part. No one is the loser." She points out that her mother would not be so critical if she were a boy.

In fact Zhenia's case is ostensibly eminently reasonable. But on the question of her relationship with her stepfather her justification becomes immediately glib and insensitive. Her mother asks if she has considered her feelings. Zhenia claims the sexual act is only an extension of her friendship for her stepfather: It takes nothing way from her mother.

"As to our kissing ... Well, you have no time for kissing anyway. And then, mother, you can't want to tie Andrey exclusively to yourself and not let him have any pleasure apart. That would be a nasty proprietary attitude. It's this grandmother's bourgeois upbringing coming up."[41]

Zhenia is described honestly. She undoubtedly expressed feelings which were shared by many young communists. She was to be denounced as the symbol of depravity by innumerable party moralists. But it is important to keep her situation in perspective. Zhenia presents the statement of the dilemma and attempts a particular way out.

Kollontai makes her own position clear: "Many of the opponents of my writings tried to impose on me an absolutely false postulate that I was preaching 'free love'. I would put it the other way. I was always preaching to the women, Make yourself free from the enslavement of love of a man."

Alexandra Kollontai never solved the dilemma in her own life. She said she "tried to combine romance and works. But it was and still is difficult for a woman to combine a profession and married life." After an early unsuccessful first marriage she entered a civil marriage with a man much younger than her, Dubenko, because he put pressure on her by saying she felt too superior to marry him. This also collapsed. A friend, Zoja, who shared her ideas called her "la derniere grande amoureuse". But Alexandra Kollontai said her "love affairs ended always in the breaking down of romance. The hour of separation was inevitable." She concluded that friendship was a more sociable emotion than sexual love.[42]

Really the importance of Alexandra Kollontai was the refusal to give comfortable stock solutions precisely because she understood the complexities of the problems.

She wrote in *The New Morality and The Working Class,* "The longer the sexual crisis lasts, the more difficult it becomes. With every attempt at a solution things became more and more difficult ... The frightened people fall from one extreme into the other, and the sexual problem remains unsolved. It would be a tremendous error to assume that only members of the economically secure classes are caught in its toils. The sexual crisis creates dramas among the working people which are no less violent or tragic than the psychological conflicts of the refined bourgeoisie."[43]

Instead of presenting people with a new formula, she thought always in terms of growth. She saw the new morality being created, not imposed, in the process of development towards a communist society. Communism was about the releasing of the potential for responsibility; it implied widening the scope for the practical self-activity of masses of people. The new morality could not be mugged up from ethical manuals of do's and don'ts. It had to come from people experiencing each other in totally new surroundings. In new situations of interaction they could make new descriptions, shapes, and boundaries.

In a letter to a young comrade she wrote, "Young comrade, you asked me what position love occupies in the proletarian idealogy. You seem surprised that in moments such as these young workers should be absorbed with questions of love and everything connected with it as much if not more than with the great problems that must be solved by the Workers Republic." She then stressed the importance of cultural revolution – the victory of Communist principles and ideas in politics and economics had to be extended and transform "old concepts of life, society, work and norms of conduct". Communism made possible "the ideal of love within comradeship". It was difficult to see this clearly now.

"At present we are going through a period of transition, but it is to be hoped that in the new proletarian morals that are developing the relations between man and woman will be based on:

1. Equality; disappearance of the overpowering masculine self-sufficiency and the servile submission of women.

2. Mutual and reciprocal recognition of rights, and disappearance of all feelings of property.

3. Fraternal sensibility, together with an art that will allow the assimilation and comprehension of the psychic developments taking place in the soul of the beloved. (In bourgeois ideology, the woman alone was expected to possess this sensibility) ..."[44]

It was here that the old impulse to fight against "social injustice", "brutality from those who had the power in their hands", and "unfairness in the sexual question" united. Here, too, appeared the determination to resist "one-man management", and the whole hierarchy of domination and subordination of the old system which made individual responsibility impossible. She understood the submission of women and "her underlying protests against the throttling of her personality", and understood, too, the "inarticulate ferment", which she gave expression in *The Workers' Opposition.*[45] The revolution was process, not accomplished fact.

Such understandings were integral to both her feminism and her communism, such understandings combined to make Alexandra Kollontai peculiarly heretical, peculiarly embarrassing, peculiarly relevant, and particularly revolutionary.

Footnotes

1 On the change of emphasis in the 1930's see Wilhelm Reich, *The Sexual Revolution*. New York 1962. Part II pp 153-269

Explanations of the New Family Policy by Soviet Theorists, in *R.U.J.* Schlesinger, *Changing Attitudes in Soviet Russia, The Family.* 1949. pp. 252-6, 266, 305-6.

Nicholas S. Timasheff, *The Attempt to Abolish the Family in Russia,* in N. W. Bell and E. F. Vogel. *A Modern Introduction to the Family.* London 1960. pp. 58-63

David and Vera Mace, *The Soviet Family.* London 1964. pp. 63, 101-2, 221-232

2 Quoted in *Isabel de Palencia,* Alexandra Kollontai. New York 1947. p 137

3. For an account of the pre-revolutionary moment see Fanina Halle, *Women in Soviet Russia,* London 1933. *de Palencia,* p 29, pp. 35-88.

4. *de Palencia,* pp. 35-58.

On bourgeois feminism see also Halle, pp 88-9, on the industrial and political action of working women see Halle pp. 83-87 and pp. 102; and L. Trotsky *History of the Russian Revolution* Vol. I London 1967, p. 116

5. See Reich, pp. 164-169, and Halle pp. 149-153.

Louise Bryant, *Six Red Months in Russia.* London 1919. pp. 132-3.

Fanina W. Halle, *Women in the Soviet East.* London 1935. pp. 180-1.

6. Schlesinger. P. 99 and p. 140.

Halle, *Women in Soviet Russia,* pp 372-6.

Reich, pp 223-8.

7. L. Trotsky, *Problems of Life.* London 1924, p. 94, pp. 50-51.

8. Schlesinger, pp. 81-101

9. S. Yakopov, *The Struggle Against Offences Rooted in the Traditional Way of Life.* 1930. In Schlesinger, p. 199

10. Reich, pp. 212-14.

11. L. Trotsky, *Problems of Life,* pp. 44-61 and pp. 88-99.

12. Reich, p. 173

13. Mace, p. 68

14. V. I. Lenin, *On The Emancipation of Women.* Moscow 1965, pp. 105-108

15. Lev Gumilevsky, *The Dogs Lane,* quoted Schlesinger, p 306

16. Lenin, *On The Emacipation of Women,* pp. 104, 101

17. See Schlesinger, pp. 16-17, 169-171

18. Kollontai, *Critique of the Feminist Movement,* Schlesinger, pp. 45-46

19. Kollontai, *The Revolution of Life and Morals,* Schlesinger, p. 49

20. Kollontai, *Communism and The Family.* London 1920. pp. 12-15 21. Halle, pp. 117-125

22. Kollontai, *The Revolution of Life and Morals,* Schlesinger, pp. 49-51

23. ibid, p. 59

24. Kollontai, *Communism and the Family,* p. 1

25. ibid, p. 16

26. Kollontai, *Free Love,* p. 124

27. e.g. V. N. Shulgin, director of the Marx-Engels Institute of Pedagogy. 1925. "There will be no school in the future communists' society ... More correctly we will all be pedagogues." quoted in Mace, p. 248. For reference to an incipient schools movement, see Louise Bryant, *Six Red Months in Russia.* London 1919. pp. 253-255

28. Kollontai, *The Workers' Opposition,* Solidarity Pamphlet No. 7, pp. 35-39. See especially her criticism of the repressive professionalism of the specialists and the authoritarian implications of one-man management. pp. 7-9, 1-3

29. Kollontai, *Free Love.* pp. 1-2

30. Angelica Balabanoff, *My Life as a Rebel.* London 1938. p. 278

31. Bryant, *Six Red Months in Russia.* p. 125

32. Louise Bryant, *Mirrors of Moscow.* New York 1923. pp. 120-121

33. Reich, p. 213.

de Palencia, p. 126

34. Bryant, *Mirrors of Moscow,* pp. 121-122

35. Balabanoff, p. 277

36. de Palencia, pp. 142-143

37. Kollontai, *Free Love,* p. 237

38. ibid, p. 243

39. de Palencia, p. 137

40. Kollontai, *The Revolution of Life and Morals,* Schlesinger, p. 59

41. Alexandra Kollontai, excerpts from *Love of Three Generations,* Schlesinger, pp. 73-74

42. de Palencia, pp. 137, 32, 160-166

43. Kollontai, *The New Morality and the Working Class,* quoted in Reich, p. 170

44. Kollontai, *Letter to a Young Comrade,* quoted in de Palencia, p. 156

45. ibid. p. 156. see also *The Workers' Opposition,* op. cit.

Made in the USA
Monee, IL
07 July 2026

56549693R00017